2.07

FUN WITH SCIENCE

by

MAE and IRA FREEMAN

©Copyright, 1956, by Mae and Ira Freeman, Copyright, 1943, by Random House, Inc. All rights reserved under International and Pan-American Copyright Conventions. Published in New York by Random House, Inc., and simultaneously in Toronto, Canada, by Random House of Canada, Limited. Library of Congress Catalog Card Number: 56-11754. Manufactured in the United States of America.

RANDOM HOUSE • NEW YORK

CONTENTS

THINGS STANDING STILL

Many of the things in the world around us are at rest. They stay where they are put. Houses, pictures on the wall, a bridge, and a sack of potatoes stay where they are because all the pushes and pulls they get from their surroundings are in balance.

When you are sitting on a chair you press down on the chair with a force of a hundred or more pounds, depending on what you weigh. At the same time, the chair must be pushing upward on your body with an equal force. Otherwise you would fall. In the same way, a table pushes up on a book lying on it, and the floor in turn pushes up on the table.

An engineer must know how to take care of all the pushes and pulls that act on things. The designer of a bridge, a skyscraper, or an automobile must figure out how to keep the forces in balance.

The experiments in this book show how laws of science explain the things that happen in our surroundings. Be sure to do all the experiments so that you can see for yourself how scientific laws work.

Lay a pencil flat on the table and it will stay just where you put it. But if you try to stand that same pencil on its point, it cannot stay in balance and will fall over. How can a tight-rope walker keep from falling? Is there any danger of the Empire State Building toppling over?

Science has the answer to such questions about balance. In every object there is a certain point where the whole weight seems to center. This point is called the **center of gravity.** If you find the center of gravity of any object, you can keep it in balance by holding it up at that point.

The center of gravity of a straight stick is right at its middle. A twelve-inch ruler can be balanced by putting your finger under it at the six-inch mark.

Stick a nail and two forks into a cork, as in the picture. Rest the nail on the rim of a drinking glass and slide the nail slowly across the rim until you find the place where the forks will not fall. When they remain balanced, you have found the center of gravity of the "flying forks." It is just where the nail rests on the glass.

Find the place where the forks will stay in balance.

The center of gravity of a thing is not always where you think it is, and sometimes you may be fooled by what you see. But you can be sure that the center of gravity of every object will always try to get as low as possible.

Get a round box that has a flat edge and can roll like a wheel. A cardboard cheese box is good for this experiment. Fasten a marble to the inside rim with a piece of tape, as in the picture. Before closing the box, make a small mark on the outside so you will know exactly where the marble is.

Place one book on another to make a slope, as the picture shows. Now hold the box near the top of the slope. Be sure that the hidden weight is just a little on the DOWNHILL side of the box. When you let the box go, it rolls down the hill as you expect.

Now set the box near the bottom of the hill, with the hidden weight a little on the UPHILL side. This time, to everybody's surprise, the box will roll UP the hill!

Here is what happened. The center of gravity of the box is not at the middle, where everybody expects it to be. Instead, it is near the edge, where you attached the marble. In both of the tests, the center of gravity went down as the box rolled. But in the second test, the whole box had to roll toward the top of the hill so that the hidden weight could go down.

After doing this experiment for your friends, open the box and show them what was done.

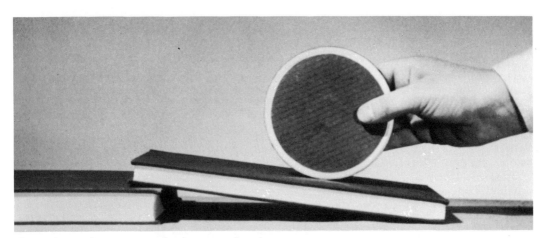

If you know how to set the box on the slope . . .

. . . it will roll uphill!

7

You know that things cannot start moving all by themselves. And when you try to move them, they seem to want to stay "as is." Scientists talk about this laziness of things by calling it **inertia.**

Suppose you are sitting in a car and the driver starts it suddenly. You fall back in your seat because the inertia of your body makes it try to stay where it is.

But it is also true that if a thing is already moving, it seems to want to keep moving. If you are riding in a car and the brakes are put on suddenly, you pitch forward because your body tries to keep going.

Test these ideas by an experiment. Place a card on top of a drinking glass, and lay a quarter on the card. Send the card flying with a sharp snap of your finger, making sure not to tip the card upward as you strike it. The quarter stays behind, as the picture shows, and falls into the glass. The inertia of the coin keeps it from going along with the card.

When the card is snapped out . . .

. . . the coin stays back.

Hang a heavy book from a doorknob with a piece of string. Tie a piece of the same string to the bottom of the book, as in the picture. Pull down evenly and steadily on the lower string. The top string will break because it was being pulled by your hand and by the weight of the book, too.

Now try the experiment again. This time, hold the lower string slack and then give it a quick downward jerk. It will break, but the upper string will not.

The inertia of the heavy book kept it from starting fast enough, and this protected the upper string.

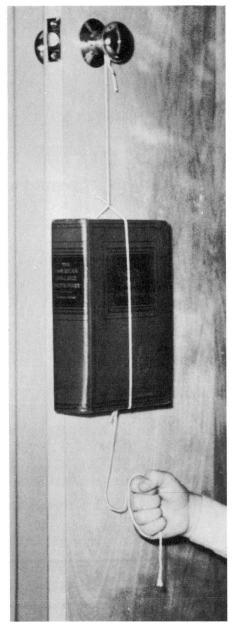

Which string will break?

10

THINGS IN MOTION

Cars whiz by on the road, birds skim through the air, elevators carry people from floor to floor in a tall building, the earth spins. All these things are moving, and the motion follows scientific laws.

The great scientist Isaac Newton watched and studied things in motion. From this he was able to form scientific laws that tell about motion of every kind.

You know that a locomotive has to pull very hard to get a train started. You also know that the train will keep moving for a long distance after the power is shut off, unless the engineer uses the brakes. Newton discovered that every moving thing wants to keep right on moving, even after you stop pushing on it.

A weight swinging around in a circle keeps trying to get away from the center. Why? What makes a rocket zoom through the air? Why does a gun kick? You can find the answers to these questions by doing the experiments on the next few pages.

If you are riding in a car going around a sharp curve in the road, you will feel as though your body is being pressed toward the outside of the curve. This is because your body tries to keep going straight ahead, but the turning of the car does not let it. Any weight that is moving swiftly around a curve tries very hard to pull toward the outside.

Get a piece of heavy string about three feet long, and pass it through the hole in a large spool. Tie one end of the string to a smaller spool and the other end to a potato.

Hold the larger spool in your hand and start the smaller spool swinging around and around in a level circle overhead. When the small spool is going fast enough, its outward-moving force will lift the much heavier potato, as in the picture.

In ancient times, long before gunpowder was invented, the catapult was an important weapon of war. It was used like a lever, making it possible to send a heavy stone through the air with great speed.

To make a catapult, place a ruler on a table with the shorter end over the edge, as in the picture. Lay a rubber eraser on the long end. Now give the short end a sharp, downward blow with your fist. The eraser will fly upward about three times as fast as your hand comes down. Can you tell why?

In trying to answer this question, notice that the part of the ruler on the table is about three times as long as the part over the edge.

12

The whirling spool lifts the heavy potato.

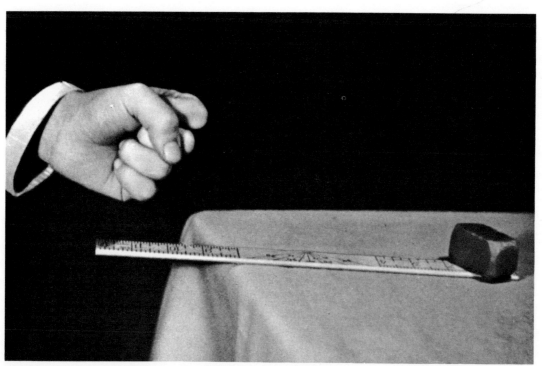

Hit the ruler with your fist and send the eraser flying.

Laws of science are used in baseball, football, bowling, tennis, and almost all other games.

In bowling, there is a rack where the returned balls line up. Whenever another ball comes along and hits the row, the ball at the far end jumps away if there is room. All the others remain perfectly still. The bump is handed on through all the balls, but only the last one is free to be knocked away.

Test this law of motion. Instead of the bowling-ball rack, use a groove formed by two rulers. For the balls, use marbles that are all the same size. Place several marbles in the groove, making sure that they touch each other. Then roll one marble toward the row with a snap of your finger. The end marble will spring away while all the others stay right where they are. If you send two marbles toward the row, just two will jump off at the other end, as in the pictures. It works this way with any number of marbles.

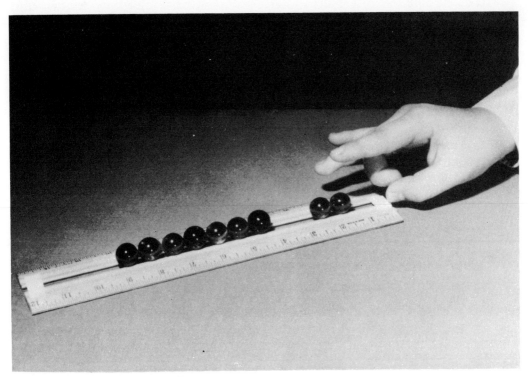

Send two marbles toward the row . . .

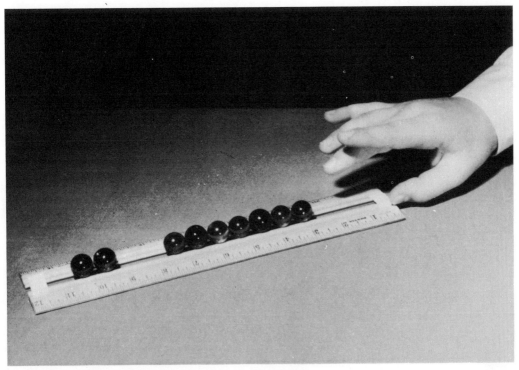

. . . and just two will jump off at the other end.

Place a broom across the top of two chairs and hang a bottle from the broomstick with two long strings. The bottle should hang level just a few inches off the floor.

Put about two tablespoons of baking soda into the bottle. Then, using a funnel, pour in about a quarter of a glass of vinegar. Now quickly cork the bottle, but not too tightly, and let it hang by the cords. In a moment or two, the cork will shoot out with a loud "pop" and the bottle will swing back, as in the lower picture.

The vinegar and baking soda formed large amounts of carbon dioxide gas inside the bottle. The gas pressed on the cork and shot it forward. But this made the bottle go in the opposite direction.

This experiment is an example of the scientific law of Action and Reaction. It shows that when anything starts moving, it must kick back on something else. You cannot have one without the other.

The law of Action and Reaction explains how rockets and jets fly. Gases shoot out of the rear of the rocket and the reaction drives the rocket itself forward. That is why a rocket can travel in outer space. It does not need to have air around to help it move.

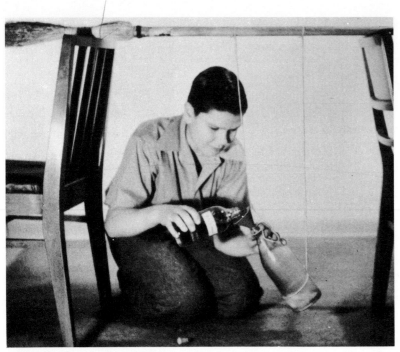

Pour in the vinegar and quickly cork the bottle.

Jet action sends the bottle backward.

Watch a stone fall from a great height. Does it drop at a steady speed, or does it fall faster and faster? Experiments prove that a falling weight will keep on gaining speed from the moment it is let go.

Test this yourself. Get a ten-foot length of string and four medium-sized potatoes. Tie a potato firmly to one end of the string. Tie another 1 foot farther along. Fasten the next one 3 feet farther on, and the last one 5 feet beyond that.

Stand on a high place and hold the free end of the string so that the lowest potato just clears the ground. Then let go. You will hear equally-spaced thumps, even though the potatoes are not at all equally-spaced along the string.

You proved that a weight takes only **twice** as long to fall 4 feet as it takes to fall 1 foot. And it takes only **three** times as long to fall 9 feet. This shows that a dropped weight keeps picking up speed at a regular rate as it falls.

Listen for the thumps as the potatoes fall.

LIQUIDS

A liquid that you pour into a dish will always settle down with its top surface perfectly level and flat. People say, "Water always seeks its level." We, as scientists, will want to know the reason for this.

A liquid presses on anything placed in it. It presses not only downward, but sideways and upward as well. Prove this easily by pushing a block of wood or empty bottle down into a pail of water. You will feel the upward push.

Because of this pressure, anything placed in a liquid seems lighter in weight. In one of the experiments you will find out why some things float in water and others do not.

Archimedes, a great Greek philosopher who lived more than two thousand years ago, discovered the law that tells about floating and sinking. Once when he was bathing in the public baths, he noticed that his body seemed to be lighter in weight when under water. He ran home at once to test the idea further, forgetting in his excitement to put on his clothes!

An understanding of liquids is needed in many branches of science and engineering.

Air must be pumped into a diver's suit to push back against the water outside. A submarine must have a strong hull to hold back the pressure of the sea. If a submarine goes too deep, it may be crushed like an eggshell.

The deeper the water, the harder it presses. The deepest spot in the ocean is about 35,000 feet down. There the water pushes with a force of nearly eight tons on every square inch.

How can a fish that lives deep in the sea stand these great pressures without being crushed? The answer is that the fish has the same amount of pressure inside its body, pushing outward. If one of these creatures is caught and hauled quickly to the surface, the inside pressure does not have time to drop to normal, and the poor fish actually blows up!

Here is an interesting way to show that the deeper the water, the harder it pushes. Use a nail to punch several holes down the side of a tin can. Put the can under a running faucet and keep it full, so that streams of water shoot from the holes.

Notice that the jets coming from the lower holes reach out farther. This shows that the push of the water is greatest near the bottom.

The deeper the water, the harder it pushes out.

A stone weighs more than a piece of wood of the same size. A quart of water weighs more than a quart of oil. Scientists say that a stone is more **dense** than wood and that water is more dense than oil. An object can float in a liquid only if it is less dense than the liquid.

To prove this, place an egg in a glass of water. If it is perfectly fresh, so that there is no gas in it, the egg will sink to the bottom. But if you dissolve two tablespoons of salt in the water, the egg will float. Adding salt makes the liquid more DENSE than the egg.

Stick a thumb tack into the end of a pencil. This weights the pencil so that it will float with the point upward, as in the picture. Make a mark on the side of the pencil where the water line comes.

Float the same pencil in a glass of strong salt water and notice that it now rides higher. This is because salt water is more dense than plain water.

In doing this experiment, you are really making an instrument called a **hydrometer.** A hydrometer is a float that is marked to tell how dense a liquid is. Service stations use this instrument to test the liquid in the battery of your car.

Which glass has salt water in it?

A home-made hydrometer.

Air pressing from the outside pushes the water up.

Stand a lighted candle firmly in the center of a soup plate with a drop of melted wax. Pour water into the plate until it is almost full.

Now place a milk bottle over the candle, as in the picture. Soon you will see the water begin to climb up inside the bottle. Then the candle flame goes out.

The flame went out when it used up some of the oxygen in the bottle. The remaining part of the air took up less room, and so the outside air was able to push up into the bottle.

WATER'S INVISIBLE SKIN

Have you ever watched drops falling from a faucet, or rain dripping from a window sill? Then you probably noticed that each drop hangs like a little rubber balloon full of water, until it breaks away. Every water surface seems to be covered with a tightly-stretched skin. This is called **surface tension.**

The scientific explanation is that the tiny molecules of water like to stick together very tightly. Because of this bunching-together, the surface of a liquid always tries to make itself as small as possible. It acts as if it were made of stretched rubber.

Surface tension shows itself clearly in a soap bubble. The water of the bubble is stretched so thin it would take a hundred thousand layers to stack up an inch high. A big bubble on an open bubble-pipe will get smaller and smaller as surface tension draws it together.

Surface tension is important in getting things clean. Most of the dirt that sticks to your clothes or your hands is held there by a thin layer of oil or grease. Soap and detergents weaken the surface tension of the grease, so that the dirt can be rinsed away.

Lay a razor blade on a dinner fork so that you can lower it carefully onto the surface of some water in a cup. The blade is made of steel and you would not expect it to float. But there it rests on top of the water, as the picture shows.

How is this possible? For the answer, look closely at the surface of the water. It curves up all around the edge of the blade. This means that the steel is resting **ON TOP** of the water and is not floating **IN** the water like a boat. Surface tension holds it up. Insects that skim over the surface of a pond are able to "walk on water" for the same reason.

When the great scientist Michael Faraday was a student, he carelessly left a towel hanging over the edge of a partly filled wash bowl. When he awoke the next morning, he was surprised to find the bowl empty and the water in a pool on the floor. Surface tension had lifted the water in the tiny spaces between the threads of the towel.

You can do Faraday's experiment yourself. Place a handkerchief in a jar of water, leaving one end hanging over the side, as in the picture. Later, you will find that surface tension has lifted the water over the edge and let it drop into the glass.

What keeps the razor blade from sinking?

Surface tension lifts the water through the handkerchief.

When soap is put into water, it weakens the surface tension. Even the tiniest bit of soap is enough to change the surface tension of a large amount of water.

To show this, sprinkle pepper evenly over some water in a clean soup plate. The pepper has no effect on the water. It is used only to make the surface easy to see.

Now touch the water near one edge of the dish with a wet bar of soap. The moment the bar reaches the water, the surface snaps back to the opposite side of the dish, as you can see by the movement of the pepper.

THROUGH THE AIR

The only time we notice air is when it is in motion. Air can do surprising things when it is moving fast. It can uproot trees, lift the roofs off houses, and cause other destruction.

If you put your hand out of the window of a moving car, you can feel the backward push of the air. Actually, your hand is moving and the air is still, but the result is the same as though you held your hand in a stream of moving air.

A leaf or a piece of paper does not crash to the ground like a stone, but drifts down slowly. It is held back by the air.

Engineers who design automobiles, airplanes, rockets and large guns must have a good understanding of the **resistance** of the air to things that move through it. The resistance depends very much on the shape of the object. **Streamlining** means shaping the object so that it will not churn up the air behind it when it moves. A streamlined airplane or train does not disturb the air very much as it passes, and so uses less power to keep it moving.

Nature is an excellent streamline engineer. Birds and fishes have streamlined shapes that let them move at high speed through the air or water with very little effort.

A balloon **floats** in the air, but an airplane will not stay up unless it keeps moving forward. An airplane seems to be held up by the stream of air under the wing. But this idea is not correct, and you can find out the true facts by doing an experiment.

Cut a strip of thick paper or light cardboard about two inches wide and one foot long. Stick the ends together with a strip of tape and curve the sides little by little until the whole loop has the shape of the side view of an airplane wing, as in the picture.

Slip a pencil through the loop and hold it in the stream of air from an electric fan. The loop will be lifted and stand out level.

Now block off the air from the top of the wing with a stiff cardboard, as shown in the second picture. As the edge of the cardboard comes near, the end of the wing drops. This proves that most of the lifting was done by the air that flowed over the TOP of the wing.

More than three-quarters of the weight of an airplane is held up by air flowing over the top of the wing, and only one-fourth by air pushing on the bottom.

It is a scientific law that anything alongside a swift stream of air or water will be pulled **INTO** the stream instead of being pushed aside as you might expect. This explains how the wing was held up by air moving swiftly across its top side.

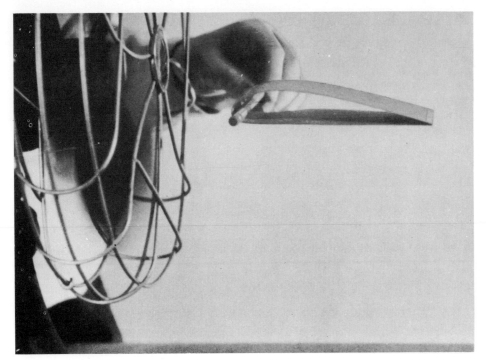

The wing flies . . .

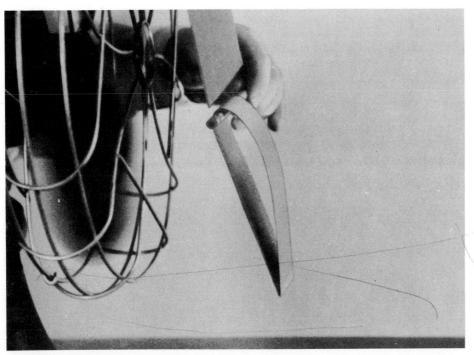

. . . until you cut off the airflow on top.

Try another experiment with moving air. Stick a pin half way through a two-inch square of light cardboard. Hold the card flat against one end of a spool with the pin inside the hole. The pin is there only to keep the card from sliding to the side.

Now blow hard and steadily through the spool and you will find that you can let the card go. It will not fall as long as there is a steady stream of air coming through the spool, even if you lean over so the spool faces downward.

The experiment with the airplane wing showed you that things are pulled **INTO** a fast-moving stream of air. Here, the card was pulled upward into the stream of air coming through the spool.

Some of the laws of science that you have been testing in this book will help you understand how a boomerang works. A boomerang is started with a sharp spinning motion, and inertia keeps it steady in its flight.

But even more important is the way that air acts on the weapon as it moves along. It forces the boomerang to slant upward as it goes, and this makes it swing in a large circle and come back to the thrower.

Make a boomerang by cutting a piece of stiff cardboard in the shape of a Y. The three arms must be the same distance from each other.

Lay the boomerang on a book with one arm of the Y over the edge, as in the picture. Tilt the book slightly upward and, with a sharp tap of a pencil, send the boomerang spinning away. It will swing around in a big circle and come back quite near to you.

The harder you blow,
the tighter it holds.

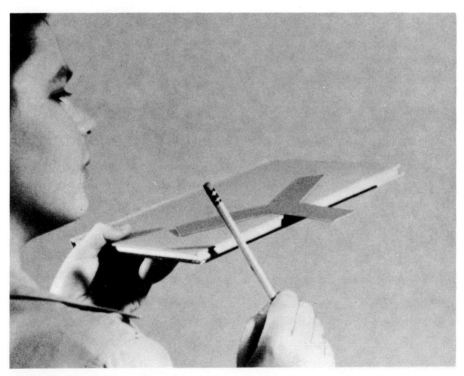

Cardboard boomerang.

Everything that falls is slowed up by the air. A big object is held back more than a small one because it must push more air aside as it falls. The huge surface of a parachute gathers enough air to slow up the fall of the load it carries.

Make a parachute by tying the corners of a handkerchief to a spool with small pieces of string all the same length. Fold the parachute around the spool and throw it into the air like a ball. The parachute will fill out in the air and float gently down. Without the parachute, the spool would dive to the ground.

34

SOUND AND MUSIC

If a stone is dropped into a quiet pond, ripples spread out in circles over the water. Science tells us that sound travels through the air in the same way, in the form of waves.

Sound waves are not exactly like those on water. The air in a sound wave has a push-and-pull motion, instead of moving up and down like the surface of water.

Any object that can shake back and forth very quickly sends out sound waves. Then we say that the object **vibrates**. If there are between 20 and 18,000 vibrations each second, your ear "hears" a sound. This means that your eardrum starts vibrating in step with the sound waves.

The main part of any musical instrument is something that can be made to vibrate. In a violin, the strings vibrate when rubbed with the bow. In playing a trumpet, the lips make the air inside the tube vibrate. Hitting a drum with sticks makes the stretched skin vibrate.

A noise is a jumble of all sorts of sound waves. A musical sound is an even set of waves, all of the same kind. The faster a thing vibrates, the higher its tone will be.

Waves act in a very surprising way. Two sets of waves coming from different places can pass right through each other without changing their shape.

Prove this to yourself by tossing two stones into a quiet pond or a large pan of water. One group of round ripples will cross directly through the other. Each will keep its shape, just as if the other were not there at all.

The same thing happens with sound waves. This explains why you can hear one person's words even though other people in the room are talking at the same time. The set of sound waves from each voice goes through the air without mixing up the others.

If you tap the side of an empty drinking glass with a pencil, it vibrates and gives off a tone. If some water is poured into the glass, the tone will be different because the part of the glass that is free to vibrate is changed in size.

You can easily set up a homemade musical instrument. Fill seven drinking glasses with different amounts of water to sound the notes of the scale. Keep adding the water slowly as you test each glass, until it gives off the proper note. Tap the glasses with a pencil to play simple songs.

Sound waves do this, too.

You can play tunes on them.

When a bell is struck, the metal vibrates and starts up sound waves in the air. A bell is only a curved piece of metal. A spoon is a curved piece of metal too, so it should be possible to get a bell-like tone by striking an ordinary spoon.

Get a tablespoon and a piece of string about five feet long. Tie the middle of the string tightly to the handle of the spoon. Hold one end of the string inside each ear with your finger, and let the spoon hang down freely, as in the picture.

Now swing the spoon gently and let it strike against a table or chair. The sound you hear is surprisingly loud and clear, just like the tone of a church bell.

The tone will seem loud only to you, and not to anyone standing near by. This is because the vibrations are carried directly to your ears through the string instead of spreading through the air.

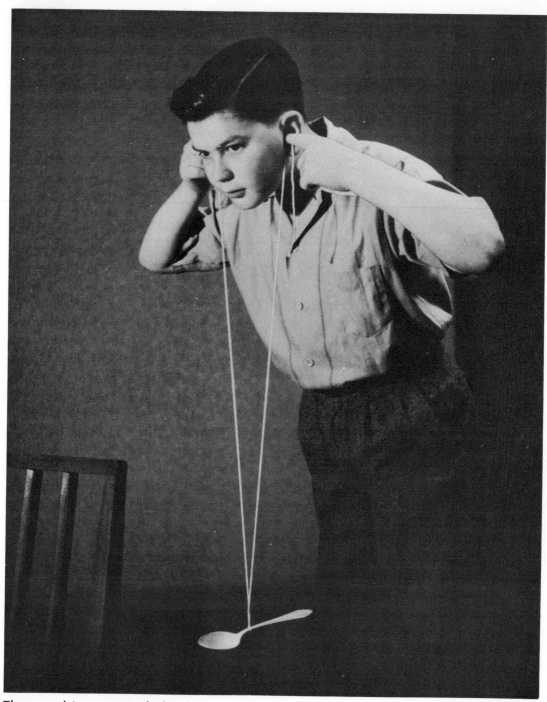
The sound is surprisingly loud.

Sound waves move through the air at a speed of about 1,100 feet a second. Light waves travel very much faster. A distant flash of lightning is seen at once, but the sound waves of the thunder arrive later. They take about five seconds to go a mile.

The next time there is a thunderstorm, figure out how far away it is. Watch for a lightning flash and then count the number of seconds from the time you see the flash until you hear the thunder. Divide this number by five, and the answer is the distance in miles. For instance, if the sound comes to you twenty seconds after you see the flash, you know that the storm is four miles away.

HOW HEAT ACTS

Heat can be carried from one place to another in different ways. First, it can pass direct from a hot object to a cold one if the two actually touch. A spoon gets hot when it is put into a pan of boiling water.

Second, heat may be carried by warmed air. A frying pan on the stove does not need to touch the flame. It gets its heat from air that is warmed by the flame and then rises to touch the pan.

Third, you can get heat from light, and that is how you are warmed by the sun's rays. In the same way we get heat from an open fire or an electric heater.

Adding or taking away heat can make great changes in materials. If you take enough heat away from water, it becomes solid. It is then ice. If you give enough heat to water, it becomes a gas. We call it steam.

Giving heat to an object will make it expand, and cooling will make it shrink. Temperature can be measured in this way. Heat makes the mercury in an ordinary thermometer expand and push its way up the stem to mark a higher temperature.

If you put one end of a metal rod in a fire, the other end very soon becomes too hot to hold in your hand. Heat is able to pass along the rod very easily because any metal is a good **conductor** of heat. Wood, cloth, plastic, and stone do not conduct heat easily. That is why pots and pans have plastic handles, and why you use a cloth to remove a hot dish from the oven.

If you touch a piece of metal and a piece of wood at the same time, the metal will feel colder than the wood, even if both are really at the same temperature. The metal feels cold because it leads heat away from your hand so quickly.

About a hundred years ago there were often bad explosions in the English coal mines. The miners used candles to light their way, and the open flames would sometimes set off gases that gathered in the mine. The great chemist, Sir Humphry Davy, thought of putting a wire cage around each candle. He figured that the metal wires would lead the heat of the flame away before it could get through to the explosive gases. The idea worked, and the "Davy safety lamp" saved the lives of many miners everywhere.

See how metal wires lead away heat. Lower a small piece of screen wire or an old wire strainer down onto a candle flame. Notice how the flame is sharply cut off, even though the screen is "full of holes."

The metal screen is "full of holes"...

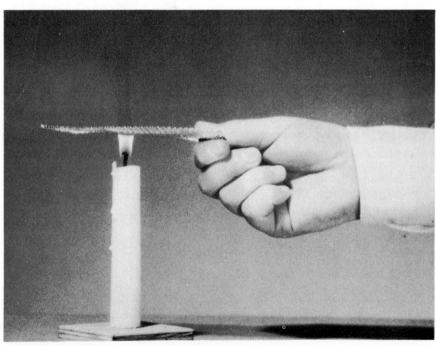

... but the flame cannot get through.

Ice melts as soon as the thermometer rises to 32 degrees. But you can make ice melt just by squeezing it!

Fill a bread pan with water and place it in the freezer. When the water is frozen through, you can remove the brick-shaped piece of ice by setting the pan in warm water for a moment.

Rest each end of the ice brick on a wooden box. Hang a loop of thin, bare wire over the middle of the ice and tie a heavy rock to the ends of the loop. Place a pail underneath the hanging rock to catch the water that drips off the ice.

Soon you will notice that the wire is cutting into the ice. After a time it cuts completely through and the rock falls into the pail. But the bar remains whole and strong.

Pressure from the wire made the ice melt where the wire touched it. The water that formed from the melted ice flowed around to the upper side of the wire and froze again, leaving the ice in one piece. The same thing happens when you "pack" a snowball. Pressure makes the snow melt. When you stop pressing, it freezes together again.

Every time you skate in winter, you make use of this unusual fact about ice. Pressure of the skate blade melts some ice for a moment, and you really glide along on a thin layer of water. In very cold weather the skating is not good because the pressure of the blade is not great enough to melt the ice.

The bar of ice remains whole after the wire cuts through.

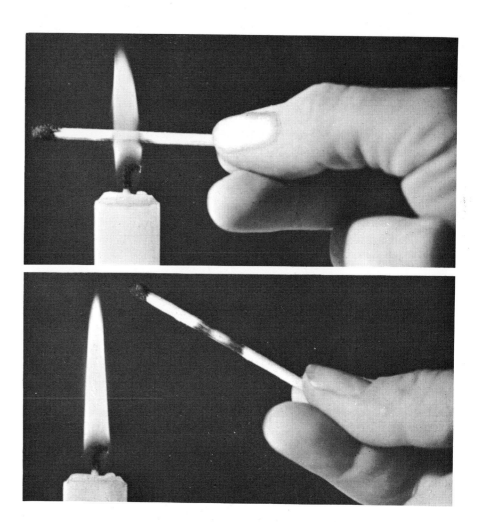

Interesting things happen inside a candle flame. Wax melts and rises in the wick. Then the wax steams off and burns where it meets the air. This means that the flame itself has a cooler inside part, with a hot layer of burning wax vapor around it.

Light a candle and keep the burned wooden match stick. When the flame is steady, slide the match stick sidewise into the flame for a moment. When you remove the stick, you will find it charred only in the two places where the hot outer layer of the flame touched it. The middle is clear because it was in the cooler inner part of the flame.

ELECTRICITY

More than two thousand years ago, people found that small bits of wool would stick to a piece of amber that had been rubbed with a cloth. The mysterious "something" on the stick of amber that made it do this was called a charge of **electricity.**

You can get a slight electric shock by touching a radiator or water faucet after walking across a woolen rug. The charge of electricity is produced by the rubbing of your shoes against the carpet.

There are many other ways to get a charge of electricity. Hold a sheet of paper and rub it briskly with the palm of your hand. Then place the paper on the wall. The paper will stick to the wall, held there by the charge you produced. Next, pull the paper away. You will hear a crackling noise which is really a small-sized electrical storm. Benjamin Franklin tried his famous kite experiment and showed that lightning is nothing but a huge electric spark.

When a charge of electricity is allowed to move along a wire, it can do many useful things. It runs motors, operates telephones, lights our homes and schools and factories, and makes possible the miracle of radio and television.

Give a comb a charge of electricity by running it through your hair quickly several times. Bring the end of the charged comb close to a thin, steady stream of water. When the comb is about an inch away, the stream will start to bend toward it. This shows that things are strongly attracted by nearby electric charges.

Be careful not to get the comb wet, or the effect will be spoiled. The least bit of moisture, even though you cannot see it, will let the charge leak away. For this reason, experiments with electric charges work best in dry weather. Touching the charged comb to the faucet will also spoil the effect, because the electricity can leak off to the ground very easily along the metal.

Sometimes friction in machinery will build up so much charge that it makes a spark and causes a fire or explosion. The way to prevent this is to get the charge away before too much of it gathers. The tires of a car, rubbing on the road, sometimes build up great amounts of charge. A special strap dragging from the axle will let the charge leak off.

A lightning rod on top of a house lets the very great charge on a cloud leak away to the ground without harming the building itself. The picture on page 40 shows a bolt of lightning striking a tall building. The steel frame of the building carries the current to the earth.

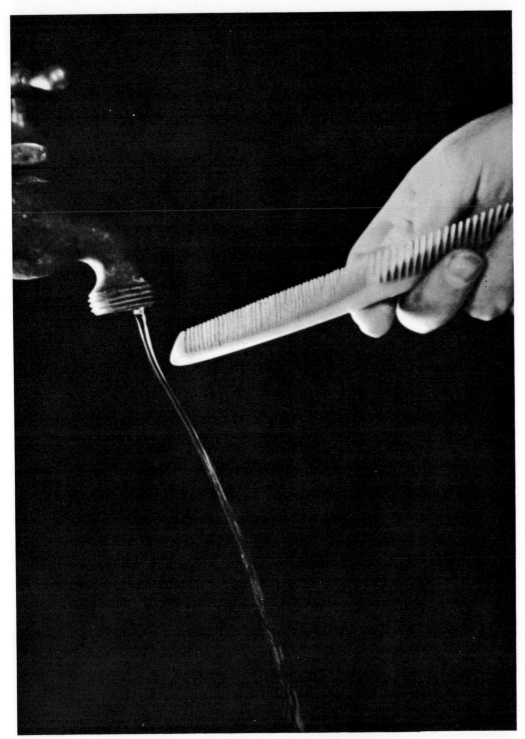

The electric charge on the comb pulls the stream of water.

When electricity flows through a wire it produces magnetism. Electric motors that run refrigerators, vacuum cleaners and other machinery work in this way. The electric current that goes into a motor produces magnetism in the coils. This magnetic force turns the motor and does useful work.

Make a lifting magnet by taking about ten feet of bell wire and winding it on a big nail. Wind one turn right next to another, making several layers, always going around the nail in the same direction. Leave about a foot of wire at each end, and keep the turns in place by fastening the ends with tape.

Tape together two flashlight cells so that the bottom of one makes good contact with the top of the other. Scrape the insulation off the ends of the wire from the coil and tape one end to the bottom of the lower cell. Dump some carpet tacks in a little pile on the table and you are ready to test your magnet.

Touch the point of the nail to the pile of tacks while you press the loose end of the wire to the top post of the cell. The nail will pick up the tacks. Lift the wire away to stop the current and the tacks will drop off.

The nail is a magnet only while the electric current is flowing in the coil. This kind of magnet is called an **electromagnet.**

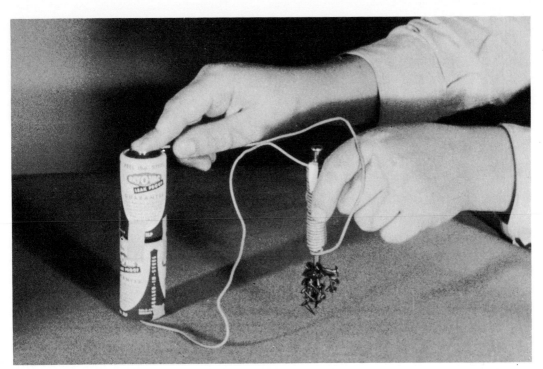

The nail is a magnet . . .

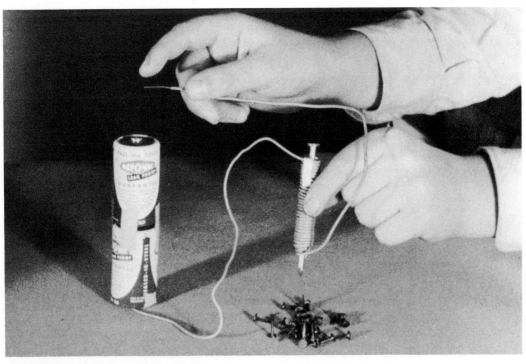

. . . only while the current is on.

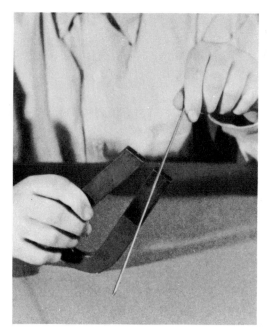
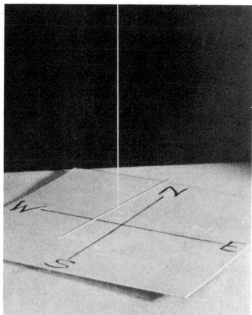

Long ago, people discovered that some rocks were natural magnets. If they hung one of these rocks so that it could turn easily, it always swung around to a north-and-south position. They did not know why this happened, but they made good use of the magnetic rocks as compasses.

We know now that a magnet always turns so as to line itself up with the north-and-south magnetic pull of the earth itself.

These days, magnets are usually made by electricity, as in the experiment with the electromagnet. But if you already have a magnet, you can make others from it without electricity. This is an easy way for you to make a compass needle.

Get a toy magnet and a steel knitting needle. Rub the needle along one end of the magnet with smooth strokes about twenty times, always rubbing in the same direction. Hang the needle by a silk thread over a card marked North, South, East and West, and you have a compass.

LIGHT AND SIGHT

Anything that glows, such as the sun, a firefly, a candle flame or a neon tube, sends out waves of light. When light waves come into your eye, you can see the thing they came from.

Not everything we see sends out its own light waves. Most things are seen by **reflected** waves. The sun shines on a house and the waves bounce off to your eye. If all the lights in a room are turned off, there are no waves to be reflected and you can see nothing in the room. Mirrors work by reflecting light in a special way.

When light hits an object, some of the waves are reflected and some may go right through the object, especially if it is transparent like water or glass.

Sunlight is a mixture of light of every color. You can see these colors when they are spread out in a rainbow.

In outer space, light travels at the amazing speed of more than 186,000 miles a second. It goes a little slower in air, water and glass, but still unbelievably fast when compared with the speed of almost everything else.

A very interesting fact about light is that it travels in straight lines. You know that it is impossible to "see around a corner" without using a trick of some kind. A carpenter sights along the edge of a board to see if it is straight. A searchlight can throw only a straight beam.

Make some shadow pictures to prove that light moves in straight lines. The boy in the photograph is holding his hands so that the shadow looks like a dog's head. Notice also that the outline of the boy's face is matched by its shadow. You can make such pictures only because light goes in straight lines.

The picture shows what happens when sun shines on a glass of milk. The curved inner side of the glass reflects the light to form a bright, crescent-shaped patch on the milk.

Any hollow curved reflector gathers and concentrates light. That is how the mirrors in telescopes are used. The glass must be curved in a very special way so that the light can be gathered at a single point. The telescope at Mount Palomar in California uses a mirror of this kind nearly seventeen feet across. It is the largest telescope mirror in the world.

When light waves go from air into water or glass, they suddenly change their direction. The reason is that light travels more slowly in water and glass, and this makes the whole beam swing aside. This bending aside of light is called **refraction.**

Hold a pencil in a bowl of water, as in the picture. Look at the pencil from above and a little to one side. The part of the pencil that is under water seems to be bent upward, because the light waves are bent aside as they come out of the water.

If you wear glasses, or if your hobby is photography, you should know something about the bending of light waves by lenses. A lens is a curved piece of glass that can bend light waves in special ways .

Water sometimes acts like a lens. Look at a tablecloth through a glass of water and notice how the weave of the cloth looks larger. A modern microscope uses sets of many lenses and can make things look thousands of times larger than they really are.

Refraction of light makes the pencil look bent.

Your eyes are wonderful little television cameras that give you an always-changing picture of the things around you. The eye has a lens inside it that gathers light on the sensitive back surface, called the **retina.** Nerves from the retina give the brain a report of what you see.

There is one spot in your eye which is blind! This is the place where the nerve bundle is joined to the retina. If any light happens to fall at this point, you will not see it.

To find the blind spot, hold this page a little more than a foot from your face. Keep your left eye closed, and look at the cross in the drawing with your right eye. You will also see the dot and the triangle.

Now keep looking at the cross with your right eye while slowly bringing the book closer. You will find a place where the triangle disappears as your view of it falls on the blind spot. Slowly move the book still closer and the dot becomes invisible but you can see the triangle again.

The **pupil** of the eye (the little round, black dot in the center) has a way of controlling how much light comes in. In bright sunlight, the pupil closes down to the size of a pinhead, letting in less light and protecting your eye from glare. In dim light, the pupil opens wide, letting in more light so that you can see clearly.

ATOMICS

Everything around us is made of **atoms** that are so tiny you would never guess they are there. Nobody has ever seen an atom, but scientists have found clever ways to count them, to weigh them, and to measure their size. If a drop of water could be enlarged to the size of the whole earth, the atoms in it would look only as big as basketballs.

Until about fifty years ago, people thought an atom was the smallest possible bit of anything. Then scientists discovered that atoms are made of **protons, neutrons** and **electrons** that are many thousands of times smaller than the atoms themselves! Every atom is made of nothing but these three things.

Most kinds of atoms stay the same all the time, but there are some that split up by themselves. Radium is one of these. When a radium atom splits, it shoots out some of the pieces with great force. This is **atomic energy.**

Scientists figured out that much more energy would come from other kinds of atoms if they could find a way to make them split. After years of study and experiments, they finally found out how to do this. From their work we now have the atom bomb, the nuclear reactor and atomic power.

Each kind of atom has a certain number of electrons in it. An electron is a tiny bit of electrical charge.

There are ways to give an atom extra electrons, or to take some away. As long as an atom has its regular number of electrons, it is just an ordinary atom. If you change the number of electrons, the atom gets an electrical charge.

You can do a scientific experiment in which you add some electrons to atoms, and then take them away again. This experiment works best when the weather is not humid.

Crumple a piece of tissue paper to form a ball the size of a marble. Cover the ball completely with a metal wrapper from a stick of chewing gum. Hang the ball by a long thread, as in the picture.

Now run a comb through your hair several times. By doing this, you are letting electrons from your hair stick to atoms of the comb. In this way the comb gets an electrical charge.

Touch the hanging ball lightly several times with the comb to let some of the electrons go over to the ball. Now the ball will back away from the comb, as the first picture shows. This happens because the electrons on the ball and the electrons that stayed on the comb push each other apart.

Now take the electrons away from the ball by holding a lighted candle under it for a moment. Immediately, the ball falls back against the comb. The reason is that there are atoms in the candle flame that have lost some electrons. As these atoms float upward and hit the ball, they grab the extra electrons away from it. In this way the ball loses its charge.

Scientists discovered cosmic rays in just this way. They noticed that the electrical charge on certain instruments kept leaking off. They traced this to the powerful cosmic rays from outer space, which kept changing the number of electrons on atoms in the air. When these atoms touched the instrument, they took away some of its charge.

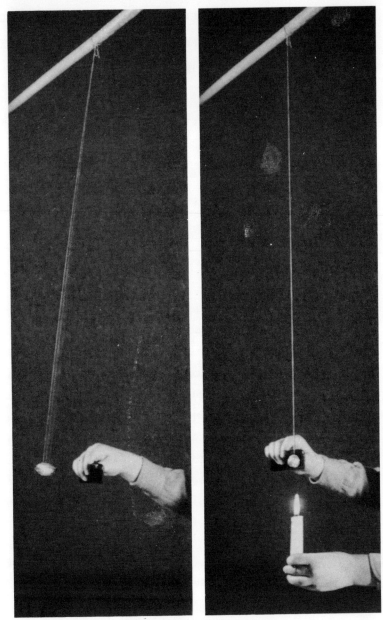

Getting rid of electrons.

The power of nuclear reactors and A-bombs comes from splitting atoms of uranium or plutonium. A stray neutron that wanders into the center of one of these atoms acts like a trigger and sets loose the energy. Scientists call this **atomic fission.**

But every time such an atom splits, it shoots out more neutrons, and some of these can make still more atoms split. One fission can cause 2 split-ups, 2 can cause 4, 4 can cause 8, and so on. This is called a **chain reaction.** The numbers double themselves again and again, and soon the total is enormous.

Do an experiment to see how a chain reaction works. Cut 20 or 30 strips of wax paper about 4 inches long and an inch wide, and crease them down the middle. Lay one strip down on a cement floor, with the sides sloping downward like a roof. From the end of this strip lay down two more, branching out in a V. From the end of each of these lay out another pair. Keep doing this until you have used all the strips. The upper picture shows how.

Now touch a lighted match to the first strip. As soon as the flame reaches the other end, it starts two strips burning. After a short while the whole set has been destroyed by this fire chain reaction.

To keep a nuclear reactor from "running away," control rods are used to block some of the flying neutrons. This breaks the chain. In the A-bomb, the action is not held back, and trillions of trillions of atoms split up in less than a thousandth of a second.

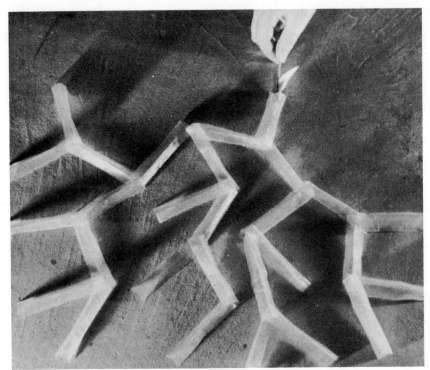

Lay out a pattern of wax paper strips.

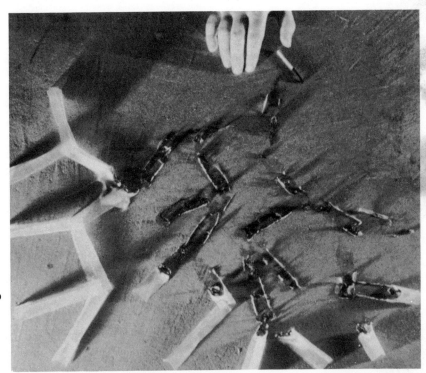

Each burning strip sets two more afire.

63

You can actually watch atoms splitting up. All you need is a fairly strong magnifying lens and a watch or clock with a luminous dial. This experiment should be done after dark.

Take the magnifying lens and the clock into a perfectly dark room, such as a cellar or closet. Wait a few minutes while your eyes get used to the dark. Then hold the lens near your eye and look closely at the numbers on the dial of the clock. You may have to move the clock back and forth a little until you see the dial sharply.

Instead of the even glow of the numbers on the dial, you will now see many flickering points of light.

The paint on the dial of your clock has a speck of radium mixed with it. Each little flash of light is caused by a radium atom splitting up, making a tiny spark in the paint material. Thousands of these flashes give the steady glow that you see without the lens.